One More River

A Traditional Spiritual

Text Adapted by Karen L. Blumen

Illustrated by John J. Blumen

Augsburg

MINNEAPOLIS

Dedicated with love to
Ross, Neil, and Kate

Melody line and complete lyrics appear on last page.

ONE MORE RIVER

Text adaptation copyright © 1995 Augsburg Fortress
Illustrations copyright © 1995 John J. Blumen

Cover and interior design: Elizabeth Boyce

Library of Congress Cataloging-in-Publication Data

Blumen, Karen, 1954–
    One more river / text adapted by Karen Blumen ; illustrations by John Blumen.
        p. cm.
    Includes words to the spiritual.
    Summary: A classic spiritual about Noah's ark adapted for reading, singing, and counting and with the melody line accompanying each verse of the song.
    ISBN 0-8066-2759-X (alk. paper)
    1. Children's songs--Texts. [1. Noah (Biblical figure)--Songs and music. 2. Noah's ark--Songs and music. 3. Animals--Songs and music. 4. Counting. 5. Songs.] I. Blumen, John, 1954–   ill. II. Title.
PZ8.3.B59865On   1995
782.25'3--dc20   95-21209
[E]   CIP
                                                                          AC

Manufactured in the U.S.A.   AF 9-2759

    99   98   97   96   95   1   2   3   4   5   6   7   8   9   10

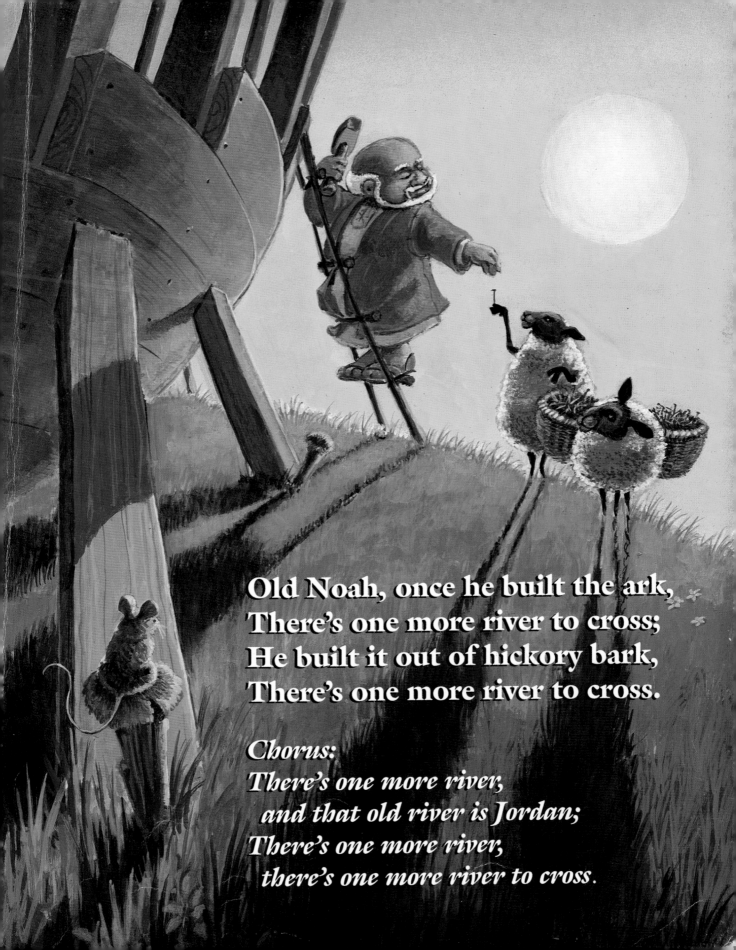

Old Noah, once he built the ark,
There's one more river to cross;
He built it out of hickory bark,
There's one more river to cross.

Chorus:
There's one more river,
  and that old river is Jordan;
There's one more river,
  there's one more river to cross.

1
one

The animals went in one by one,
There's one more river to cross;
The elephant chewin' a caraway bun,
There's one more river to cross.

Chorus:
There's one more river,
    and that old river is Jordan;
There's one more river,
    there's one more river to cross.

2
two

The animals went in two by two,
There's one more river to cross;
The crocodile and the kangaroo,
There's one more river to cross.

Chorus:
There's one more river,
   and that old river is Jordan;
There's one more river,
   there's one more river to cross.

3
three

The animals went in three by three,
There's one more river to cross;
The bear, the flea, and the bumblebee,
There's one more river to cross.

Chorus:
> There's one more river,
>   and that old river is Jordan;
> There's one more river,
>   there's one more river to cross.

4
four

The animals went in four by four,
There's one more river to cross;
The big hippopotamus stuck in the door,
There's one more river to cross.

Chorus:
There's one more river,
and that old river is Jordan;
There's one more river,
there's one more river to cross.

5
five

The animals went in five by five,
There's one more river to cross;
With Saratoga trunks they did arrive,
There's one more river to cross.

Chorus:
    There's one more river,
        and that old river is Jordan;
    There's one more river,
        there's one more river to cross.

6
six

The animals went in six by six,
There's one more river to cross;
The hyena laughed at the monkey's tricks,
There's one more river to cross.

Chorus:
*There's one more river,
    and that old river is Jordan;
There's one more river,
    there's one more river to cross.*

7
seven

The animals went in seven by seven,
There's one more river to cross;
Said the ant to the antelope,
   "Who are you shovin' ?"
There's one more river to cross.

Chorus:
   There's one more river,
      and that old river is Jordan;
   There's one more river,
      there's one more river to cross.

8
eight

The animals went in eight by eight,
There's one more river to cross;
Some were early and some were late,
There's one more river to cross.

Chorus:
*There's one more river,
     and that old river is Jordan;
There's one more river,
     there's one more river to cross.*

9
nine

The animals went in nine by nine,
There's one more river to cross;
Old Noah shouted, "Cut that line!"
There's one more river to cross.

Chorus:
> *There's one more river,*
> *and that old river is Jordan;*
> *There's one more river,*
> *there's one more river to cross.*

10
ten

The animals went in ten by ten,
There's one more river to cross;
If you want any more,
    you can read it again,
There's one more river to cross.

Chorus:
*There's one more river,
    and that old river is Jordan;
There's one more river,
    there's one more river to cross.*

One More River

Verse: Old No - ah, once he built the ark, There's one more ri - ver to cross;
He built it out of hick - ory bark, There's one more ri - ver to cross.

Chorus: There's one more riv - er, and that old riv - er is Jor - dan;

There's one more riv - er, there's one more riv - er to cross. ____

Old Noah, once he built the ark,
There's one more river to cross;
He built it out of hickory bark,
There's one more river to cross.

Chorus:
    There's one more river,
      and that old river is Jordan;
    There's one more river,
      there's one more river to cross.

The animals went in one by one,
There's one more river to cross;
The elephant chewin' a caraway bun,
There's one more river to cross. **(Chorus)**

The animals went in two by two,
There's one more river to cross;
The crocodile and the kangaroo,
There's one more river to cross. **(Chorus)**

The animals went in three by three,
There's one more river to cross;
The bear, the flea, and the bumblebee,
There's one more river to cross. **(Chorus)**

The animals went in four by four,
There's one more river to cross;
The big hippopotamus stuck in the door,
There's one more river to cross. **(Chorus)**

The animals went in five by five,
There's one more river to cross;
With Saratoga trunks they did arrive,
There's one more river to cross. **(Chorus)**

The animals went in six by six,
There's one more river to cross;
The hyena laughed at the monkey's tricks,
There's one more river to cross. **(Chorus)**

The animals went in seven by seven,
There's one more river to cross;
Said the ant to the antelope,
    "Who are you shovin'?"
There's one more river to cross. **(Chorus)**

The animals went in eight by eight,
There's one more river to cross;
Some were early and some were late,
There's one more river to cross. **(Chorus)**

The animals went in nine by nine,
There's one more river to cross;
Old Noah shouted, "Cut that line!"
There's one more river to cross. **(Chorus)**

The animals went in ten by ten,
There's one more river to cross;
If you want any more, you can read it again,
There's one more river to cross. **(Chorus)**